THE 100 GREATEST KIDS RIDDLES OF ALL TIME

The 100 Greatest Kids Riddles of All Time

www.victor-junior.com

1st Edition, 2020
Innovate Publishing
www.innovatepublishing.ca

ISBN (Paperback): 978-1-7774451-8-8

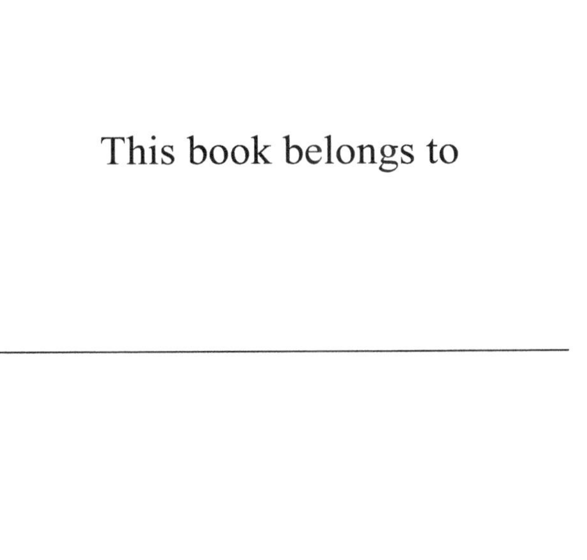

This book belongs to

____

DO YOU ACCEPT THE CHALLENGE?

The 100 Greatest Kids Riddles of All Time
gets more challenging as you go through the book.

So try your best to solve the riddles in order
and don't be afraid to ask friends and family for help.

(But just in case, all answers are at the back of the book)

GOOD LUCK - IT'S GO TIME!

1.

What Am I?

I can swim for miles.
I'm big with thick,
white hair.
I live in the Arctic.

2.

What do you have to crack before you can use it?

3.

Easton's parents have three sons.

Their names are Snap, Crackle and ____?

4.

Find one word that can connect with the following words:

Cream, Cube, Skate

5.

What gets wetter the more it dries?

6.

What Am I?

I have a face
and two hands,
but no arms
and no legs.

7.

What begins with T, ends with T, and has T in it?

8.

Can you solve the word riddle?

MYANTSPANTS

9.

What speedy vehicle is spelled the same forwards and backward?

10.

Can you solve the word riddle?

11.

What Am I?

I always go up,
but can never
come down?

12.

What begins with “E”, but only has one letter?

13.

What word is spelled wrong in every dictionary?

14.

What Am I?

I have lots of words,
but never speak.

15.

What gets bigger the more you take away?

16.

What Am I?

I'm full of holes,
but can still hold water.

17.

Where do you find keys that won't work in any lock?

18.

Can you solve
the word riddle?

19.

Choose the correct sentence:

"The yolks of the eggs is white"

or

"The yolks of the eggs are white"

20.

What Am I?

I can travel around the world without ever leaving the corner.

21.

What has four legs but can't walk?

22.

Can you solve the word riddle?

Y
R
R
U
H

23.

What has teeth, but can't bite?

24.

What Am I?

I'm as light as a feather, but even the strongest person can only hold me for 5 minutes.

25.

What Am I?

I’m tall when I’m young
and I’m short
when I’m old.

26.

What has a neck, but no head?

27.

What type of cheese is made backward?

28.

In a year, there are twelve months. Seven months have thirty-one days. How many months have twenty-eight days?

29.

Can you solve the word riddle?

30.

How many letters are there in the alphabet?

31.

When does Friday come before Thursday?

32.

What gets harder to catch the faster you run?

33.

Can you solve the word riddle?

gseg

egsg

sgeg

34.

Maya threw a ball
as hard as she could
and it came straight
back to her.

Nothing touched it and
nobody threw it back.

How?

35.

An electric train is traveling north and the wind is blowing from the east.

Which direction is the smoke blowing?

36.

What Am I?

I happen once in a minute, twice in a moment, but never in a thousand years.

37.

What Am I?

You can catch me,
but never throw me.

38.

Where can you find cities, towns, shops, and streets - but no people?

39.

What 5-letter word becomes shorter when you add two letters to it?

40.

Can you solve the word riddle?

JOBINJOB

41.

A rooster is sitting in the center of a barn roof. The wind is blowing east. If it laid an egg, would the egg roll down the left or right side of the roof?

42.

What has a bed but never sleeps, can run but never walks, and has a bank but no money?

43.

What Am I?

The more you take the more you leave behind.

44.

Who can shave 25 times a day but still have a beard?

45.

Which weighs more:

one pound of feathers

or

one pound of bricks?

46.

What Am I?

Everyone has it,
but no one can lose it.

47.

What Am I?

You'll find me in Earth,
Jupiter, Mercury,
Uranus and Mars,
but not in Venus
or Neptune.

48.

There was a one-story blue house. Inside was a girl wearing a blue dress, a boy wearing a blue shirt, a blue dog with a blue collar, a blue cat, a blue kitchen, a blue chair, a blue TV, and a blue bathroom. Everything was blue. What colour were the stairs?

49.

Can you solve the word riddle?

50.

What Am I?

You see me in the middle of March and April, but not again until the end of September?

51.

If a red house is made out of red bricks, a blue house is made of blue bricks and a yellow house is made of yellow bricks, what is a green house made of?

52.

Two mothers and two daughters went out for dinner.

Everyone ate one burger, but only three burgers were eaten in total.

How is that possible?

53.

Take away my first letter and I sound the same.

Take away my last letter and I sound the same.

Take away my middle letter and I sound the same.

What 5-letter word am I?

54.

What 5-letter word can be pronounced the same even with 4 letters are removed?

55.

How many of each species of animal did Moses take on the ark?

56.

Jax the farmer has sixteen cows and all but nine die.

How many are left?

57.

What has a head and tail, but no body?

58.

Can you solve the word riddle?

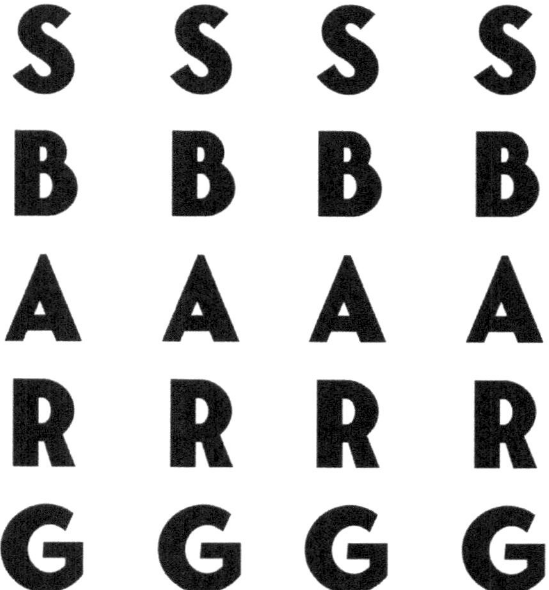

59.

A cowboy named Kai rides
into town on Monday,
stays for two days,
then leaves on Monday.
How is that possible?

60.

Who is bigger:

Mr. Bigger,
Mrs. Bigger,
or their baby?

61.

Find one word that can connect with the following words:

Cake, Swiss, Cottage

62.

What am I?

I exist when there is light,
but direct light
will kill me.

63.

What is as hard as a rock, but melts in hot water?

64.

What do the numbers 11, 69, and 88 have in common?

65.

Can you solve the word riddle?

LEV

EL

66.

A father and son were in an accident and rushed to the hospital.

The emergency doctor saw the boy and said, "*I cannot operate on this boy. He is my son.*"

How could that be?

67.

What Am I?

You can serve me, but never eat me.

68.

When Xavier was 8, his sister Lulu was half his age.

Now, Xavier is 14.

How old is Lulu?

69.

Bardot is running a race.

At the very end she passes the person in 2nd place.

What position did Bardot finish the race?

70.

Max was born in 2010,
but died in 2017
at the age of 49.

How is that possible?

71.

Can you solve the word riddle?

72.

Emma finds 3 apples in a basket and she takes 2 away.

How many apples does Emma have?

73.

What Am I?

If I have it,
I don't share it.
If I share it,
I don't have it.

74.

Duke's mother has four sons.

Their names are Fee, Fi, Fo and ____?

75.

Find one word that can connect with the following words:

Glasses, Screen, Day

76.

What goes away as soon as you talk about it?

77.

What has two hands, but cannot clap?

78.

Daniel the butcher is 5'10" tall.

What does he weigh?

79.

Can you solve the word riddle?

SITTING

THE WORLD

80.

What is at the end of a rainbow?

81.

If you throw a blue rock into the Red Sea, what will it become?

82.

What belongs to you but other people use it more than you?

83.

Name three consecutive days without using Wednesday, Friday, or Sunday.

84.

Can you solve the word riddle?

GIVE GET
GIVE GET
GIVE GET
GIVE GET

85.

What has two heads, four eyes, six legs and a tail?

86.

What is easy to get into, but hard to get out of?

87.

Pasha and Parsa are identical twins.

They have the same mother, the same father, they were born at the same hospital, but they were born on different days and in different years.

How is that possible?

88.

What Am I?

I'm a type of dress,
but I can never be worn.

89.

What Am I?

I cannot speak.
I cannot hear.
You see me and I see you.
I will always tell
you the truth.

90.

Mister Red lives in the Red House. Mister Blue lives in the Blue House. Mister Black lives in the Black House. Who lives in the White House?

91.

A bus driver is going the wrong way down a one-way street. He passes a police officer, but he doesn't stop him. Why not?

92.

Can you solve the word riddle?

93.

Find one word that can connect with the following words:

Knife, Fly, Cup

94.

Ever has $33.00.

She buys 6 books
that cost $3.00 each,
5 boxes of pencils that
cost $2.00 each
and she spends the rest
of her money on pens.

How much money did
she spend on pens?

95.

I am a 3-digit number.
My second digit is 4 times bigger than the third digit.
My first digit is 3 less than my second digit.
What number am I?

96.

If four people can repair four bicycles in four hours, how many bicycles can eight people repair in eight hours?

97.

How far can a squirrel run into the woods?

98.

What are the next three letters in the following sequence?

J, F, M, A, M, J, J, A, S, ___, ___, ___

99.

A plane crashes exactly on the border between the United States and Canada.

Where would you bury the survivors?

100.

You are driving a yellow bus. At the first stop, two red-haired women get on. The second stop, three brown-haired men get on and one black-haired woman gets off. At the third stop, three blonde-haired kids and their blonde-haired mom get on. What color is the bus driver's hair?

ANSWERS

1. A polar bear
2. An egg
3. Easton
4. Ice
5. A towel
6. A clock
7. A teapot
8. Ants in my pants
9. Racecar
10. Growing older
11. Your age
12. Envelope
13. Wrong
14. A book
15. A hole
16. A sponge
17. On a piano
18. Street corner
19. Neither. Egg yolks are yellow.
20. A stamp
21. A table
22. Hurry up
23. A comb (or a zipper)
24. Your breath
25. A candle
26. A bottle
27. Edam
28. All of them
29. Top Secret
30. Eleven: T-H-E A-L-P-H-A-B-E-T

31. In the dictionary
32. Your breath
33. Scrambled eggs
34. Maya threw the ball straight up
35. There is no smoke. It's an electric train.
36. The letter "M"
37. A cold
38. A map
39. Short (short + er)
40. In-between jobs
41. Neither. Roosters can't lay eggs
42. A river
43. Footsteps
44. A barber
45. They weigh the same
46. Your shadow
47. The letter "R"
48. There were no stairs. It was a one-story house.
49. Center of gravity
50. The letter "R"
51. Glass
52. They were a grandmother, mother, and a daughter.
53. Empty
54. Queue
55. None. It was Noah's ark.
56. Nine
57. A coin
58. Up for grabs
59. His horse's name was Monday
60. The baby - because she is a little bigger.
61. Cheese
62. A shadow
63. An ice cube

64. They read the same right side up and upside down
65. Split level
66. The doctor was his mother
67. A tennis ball
68. Lulu is 10. (Half of 8 is 4, so Lulu is 4 years younger. So when Xavier is 14, Lulu is 4 years younger, so she is 10)
69. She finished in 2nd place
70. Max was a dog (1 year = 7 dog years)
71. Two wrongs don't make a right.
72. 2 apples. (She took 2 apples away and left 1 in the basket.)
73. A secret
74. Duke
75. Sun
76. Silence
77. A clock
78. Meat
79. Sitting on top of the world
80. The letter "W"
81. Wet
82. Your name
83. Yesterday, Today, and Tomorrow
84. Forgive and forget
85. A cowboy riding a horse
86. Trouble
87. They were born on December 31 and January 1. (Two different days and two different years)
88. An address
89. A mirror
90. The President
91. Because the bus driver is walking.
92. Split Pea Soup
93. Butter
94. $5.00

95. 141

96. Sixteen

97. Halfway. After that, it is running out of the woods.

98. O, N, D (The first letter of the months of the year.)

99. Nowhere. You don't bury survivors.

100. Whatever color your hair is. You're the bus driver.

FROM THE AUTHOR

Thanks for reading *The 100 Greatest Kids Riddles of All Time.*

I hope you, your friends, and your family enjoyed it!

As a small business and self-employed writer, my Amazon review rating means everything for my success and continued growth.

If you can spare a few moments to leave a positive Amazon review it would go a long way towards helping others decide about my books.

Thank you and I look forward to seeing you again in the next book!

vj.

CHECK OUT OUR OTHER TITLES:

THE 100 FUNNIEST KIDS JOKES OF ALL TIME

THE 100 GREATEST KNOCK KNOCK JOKES OF ALL TIME

THE 100 GREATEST DAD JOKES OF ALL TIME

THE 100 GREATEST PARENTING JOKES OF ALL TIME

100 *MORE* OF THE GREATEST DAD JOKES OF ALL TIME

www.ingramcontent.com/pod-product-compliance
Lightning Source LLC
Chambersburg PA
CBHW061743050726
47598CB00002B/575